THE LAND
OF THE LONG
WHITE CLOUD

2003-2004 NMI
MISSION EDUCATION RESOURCES

❊ ❊ ❊

READING BOOKS

THE FAR SIDE OF THE SEA
From the Philippines to Ukraine
by Lynn DiDominicis

FLOODS OF COMPASSION*
Hope for Honduras
by Paul Jetter

IMPACT!*
Work and Witness Miracles
by J. Wesley Eby

THE JAGGED EDGE OF SOMEWHERE*
by Amy Crofford

THE LAND OF THE LONG WHITE CLOUD
Nazarenes in New Zealand
by Connie Griffith Patrick

SECOND WIND
Running the Race in Retirement
by Sherry Pinson

*Youth Books

❊ ❊ ❊

ADULT MISSION EDUCATION RESOURCE BOOK

CALLED TO GO
Edited by Wes Eby

THE LAND
OF THE LONG
WHITE CLOUD

Nazarenes in New Zealand

by
Connie Griffith Patrick

Nazarene Publishing House
Kansas City, Missouri

Copyright 2003
by Nazarene Publishing House

ISBN 083-412-0194

Printed in the United States of America

Editor: J. Wesley Eby
Cover Design: Michael Walsh

10 9 8 7 6 5 4 3 2 1

Dedication

This book is dedicated to the people who in response to God's grace, and joyously unaware of their sacrifice, gave of whatever gifts they possessed to the growing of the Church of the Nazarene in New Zealand.

Since a small girl, Connie has loved words. She grew up as a missionary kid in New Zealand where her parents, Roland and Dorothy Griffith, pioneered the work of the Church of the Nazarene. From the time they returned to the States when Connie was 15, she dreamed of writing a book of her childhood titled *Kiwi by Adoption*. But instead God has led her to intertwine childhood memories with a brief overview of how God has used the people called Nazarenes during the past 50 years in New Zealand.

Pasadena College (now Point Loma Nazarene University) was her choice for an institution of higher learning. There she found and married Bill Patrick, who has become her lifelong partner and friend. After graduation Connie taught school and Bill served in the U.S. Army. By then their oldest son, Kirk, was on the way, and 2½ years later, Sean was born.

Connie's public school career was terminated, but teaching was not. For 32 years her love has been teaching Bible studies and Sunday School classes. To supplement the family income, Connie worked in the cosmetic business for 16 years, teaching women how to care for their skin.

In 1993, after Bill taught high school for 20 years, he and Connie served as NIVS (Nazarenes in Volunteer Service) for 7 years in Papua New Guinea, Albania, European Nazarene College in Switzerland, and Kosovo. At the present the Patricks are residing at their home in Auburn, California.

Connie has previously written two NMI reading books: *Windows to Albania* (1998) and *The Miracle Goes On* (2000).

Contents

NEW
ZEALAND

Whangarei

Auckland • Papakura

Hamilton

Tasman Sea

NORTH
ISLAND

Wellington

Wainuiomata

Canterbury Plains

Christchurch

Pacific
Ocean

SOUTH
ISLAND

Invercargill

Introduction

November 2000

"That trunk doesn't fit in your formal living room," my sister, the interior decorator, advised. At first glance I had to agree. The brown leather was cracked, scarred, and stained from many miles. Someone had even dripped paint down one side.

I deliberately pulled the fringed edge of the cloth covering to one side to reveal the black-stenciled letters—**R. E. Griffith, Box 2912, New Zealand.** "It's my roots, my history, part of who I am. The trunk stays."

Perhaps it was that day, that conversation, that stoked the long-glowing coals of desire to write *The Land of the Long White Cloud*.

March 2001

I'm sitting at the wharf where the Aorangi of the Matson Shipping Line docked almost exactly 50 years ago. The rustic dock, blackened tugboats, and grubby sheds have been replaced with brick paving, elegant sailboats, and "high-end" quayside cafes.

I order a cup of English breakfast tea and listen to the water lapping at the piers in chorus with the memories lapping at my soul. Mostly they gently ebb and wane, but now and then they roll in with enough force to cause a quiet splash. My eyes fill

9

The wharf where the Aorangi docked in 1951

with the overflow; the brine splashes on my note-book, blurring the ink.

I'm in New Zealand to research not only my memories but also those of people who were here at the beginning, near the beginning, and now—in hopes that a new generation will catch the spirit of self-sacrifice, hard work, faith vision, and high pur-pose in service of a high and holy God.

I ask you, the reader, to make the mental shift between past and present, musings and personal memories, that together we may take a journey through time and space to learn whatever God longs to teach us from His story in New Zealand. Come!

1

The Wind in Our Sails

April 1951. Three weeks restricted to a tiny cabin and the third-class deck seemed an interminable time to a 6-year-old. Day after day, I wondered how there could be that much water anywhere. For my parents who never wasted anything, especially anything as valuable as time, it was an opportunity to share the Good News. They asked permission from the ship's captain to have children's meetings on the deck, then gathered the little ones to tell them that Jesus says, "Come."

Jesus says, "Come to Me" and "Go to all the world and teach all that I have commanded you." And we were going—with the wind in our sails.

1954. I sat in my school classroom, my 9-year-old imagination enthralled by the teacher's New Zealand history lesson. I've never forgotten the story.

"Aotearoa!" The Maori chieftain's voice strained to make his cry heard across the troubled water to the other outrigger canoes. At the start of the journey, their arms and voices had been strong. Now they were weakened by endless days in treacherous

waters, fighting life-threatening storms, suffering from dehydration, and near starvation.

"Aotearoa!" the cry came again. Finally the power of the phrase penetrated their dulled consciousnesses. With heads thrown back and throats open in joyous echo, they welcomed their journey's end. "Aotearoa! Aotearoa! Land of the Long White Cloud."

My mind returned to the day in 1951 when my family, the first explorers of the Church of the Nazarene, set foot on this land. We, like the early Polynesians, also found it covered with clouds, but this time the clouds were gray. For me, the sun-loving child of these fledgling missionaries, it seemed a bit dismal and dreary, but even dreary could not dim the sense of adventure.

○   ○   ○

The island city was damp and cold,
and the essence of Britain hung in the air.

○   ○   ○

Making our way up Queen Street from the quay at 7:00 A.M., it seemed we made an interesting trio to passersby. My 49-year-old, preacher-builder father was of larger build than the average New Zealander, and my nurse-musician mother was raising her first child in her middle years. At that time American accents were a rarity, its pronunciation strong compared to the soft sounds of New Zealand English.

Sandwiched between my parents, I tried valiantly to match my stride with theirs, for the quizzical glances of people were almost as intimidating as the gray-stone buildings on either side. The island city was damp and cold, and the essence of Britain hung in the air. The vehicles were also like those of its mother country and likewise driven on the left side of the road.

Even with the diversions, it was a long way for a 6 year-old to walk, and the grade was increasing. I tried not to complain because I knew my parents had to find a place to stay. Our baggage must be removed from the dock by 4:00 that afternoon.

I felt my parents' uncertainty. What did God have in store? Who would befriend them? Where and how would they begin? But I knew the hands that held mine. Their uncertainty was mixed with anticipation. They had come to this land on the underside of the earth, knowing no one, and yet their hearts were at rest, for they believed God had sent them. It had taken awhile for them to be convinced, but now they could see God had been working from the moment He had planted the idea through a man named George Ronnekamp.

George was preparing to fulfill God's call to preach when World War II broke out. Feeling he should do his part, he enlisted and was eventually assigned to the San Francisco Bay area as a welder in the shipyards. Roland Griffith was the pastor of the Nazarene Church in nearby Richmond. He offered George a place to rent and a place to serve, and George gladly accepted both. In the many hours helping to build the church, George saw his pastor model faith and courage with a work ethic to match. Though a solid friendship formed, contact was lost when George's ship sailed to the South Pacific. Docking twice in Auckland, New Zealand, the beauty of the country and warmth of the people made a deep impression on George. A priest visited the ship, and George asked if there was any church representing the holiness message. "Only The Salvation Army," the priest answered.

The war over, George returned to Bethany Nazarene College (now Southern Nazarene University), and after graduating took a pastorate in Hemingford, Nebraska. He felt he should invite his former pastor

The Griffiths before going to New Zealand, 1950

to come and hold a revival. Sitting around the kitchen table one evening, Rev. Griffith asked a question that would impact the future of many. "George, I like digging out new churches where people need to find Jesus Christ. My heart is drawn overseas, yet I feel that with nearly 30 years of preaching invested, I don't want to have to learn a new language at this time in my life. You've been around the world during the war. If you were me, where would you go?"

○ ○ ○

A multicolored memory of the Land of the Long White Cloud flooded George's mind.

○ ○ ○

A multicolored memory of the Land of the Long White Cloud flooded George's mind, and a knowing smile lit his face. "Go to New Zealand!"

My father did not immediately catch George's excitement. New Zealand seemed at the end of the earth, in fact nearly 9,000 miles from home. But in March 1951, a postcard arrived at the Ronnekamp's home. On one side was a picture of a ship, on the other this message: "We are on our way to New Zealand, Rolly Griffith."

Now the Griffiths were here, doing their best to obey God, knowing He would give direction at the right time.

Just when I felt I could go no farther, we spotted a lovely, old, white wooden building ahead. The stone buildings had been left behind, and the gray sky was beginning to blue. The sign at the driveway stated: The People's Palace—The Salvation Army. We made our way up the steps to the front door. The veranda was bordered with bright-colored pansies that seemed a perfect fit with the cheerful face that welcomed us inside.

Gratefully we followed her to a simple but pristine room. She gave us the details: "Meals are included in the tariff. Breakfast is served at 6, morning tea at 10, lunch at half past 12, afternoon tea at 3, and tea* is at 5 o'clock sharp." I noticed my parents nodding a bit numbly and wondered how my dad would survive with only tea for dinner. This was the first of many cultural differences.

In due time we were introduced to Major John Mahaffey, the officer in charge of the Auckland Salvation Army Corps. A connection of kindred spirits was made. We rejoiced in our common bond: the belief that a holy life could be lived here and now by the power of the Holy Spirit. Major Mahaffey asked Dad to speak for a week at the Auckland Citadel. The first night he preached on Acts 19:2, "Did you receive the Holy Spirit after you believed?" Many came forward in response to the holiness messages.

Major Mahaffey was convinced this message needed to be heard all over New Zealand. He went to his authorities to recommend "these Nazarenes," and wherever we went The Salvation Army gave us an

---

*In New Zealand the evening meal is also referred to as "tea."

open door. Youth for Christ and other independent groups were also willing to hear the American preacher and his heartwarming message. Dad preached; Mother and I sang. Our duets were augmented by her accordion; my lack of height by a chair.

Before the year's end, they had held 26 meetings, 7 to 14 days in length. Before we could finish in one town, our hosts would say, "I've a brother or friend in such and such a place. You must go there also." Wherever we went, my folks asked for the privilege of sharing God's message with the people.

"The gathering of souls has been remarkable," Dad reported. "More than 1,000 adults and children have responded to appeals to pray about their spiritual needs."

One letter my parents sent back to the States showed their concern over conserving the results of their labor. "Is there anything we can do to channel the harvest—people without the holiness message—into a fellowship to continue their growth?"

○ ○ ○

**The only constant was "change" itself—
and my very own bag of books.**

○ ○ ○

That year was also an important time of cultural orientation for our family. My memories of that first year in New Zealand are kaleidoscopic: Night after night listening to Dad's sermons . . . staying in homes . . . meeting nice people . . . beautiful flower

On the "metal" road

gardens . . . rough "metal" (gravel) roads . . . unsurpassed scenery . . . survival camping—our only meat, the game we could kill . . . scary bridges . . . mountain passes . . . Mother teaching correspondence school lessons in the car . . . memorizing despised multiplication tables . . . Dad interrupting to show me some wonderful sight . . . hundreds of morning teas, afternoon teas, teas, and 9 P.M. suppers with tea . . . in winter, wearing overcoats inside homes . . . cuddling hot water bottles in icy beds . . . in spring, summer, and autumn, the whole world in bloom . . . Dad sneezing and blowing, hardly able to drive.

But drive we did, from the northernmost parts of the North Island to Invercargill of the South Island, the closest port to Antarctica. Every day was different. We ministered in tearooms and town halls, school assemblies and church sanctuaries, Salvation Army Halls and youth camps. No place was too big or too small. The only constant was "change" itself—and my very own bag of books.

During those months Mother and Dad saw the great need for another holiness work in the land. New Zealand had two distinct people groups. Pake-ha Kiwis (people of European descent) and Maoris.* They have since been joined by a large influx of Asians. If these cultures with their unique gifts and characteristics together could be redeemed for Christ, they could turn their world upside down.

My parents talked and prayed. Since the 1952 General Assembly of the Church of the Nazarene was near, Dad purchased a plane ticket for the United States. The purpose? To present the need for opening a work of the church in New Zealand, offering themselves as pioneer "home missionaries." Mother was critically ill with pneumonia and could not travel. Placing her and me in the care of Major Jones, Dad packed his bag and was on his way without us. What would our future be?

Knowing my father, part of the 16 hours over the Pacific Ocean was spent mentally reviewing the events that had brought him to this day. Only 18 months earlier the future had looked rather bleak. My parents had returned from a yearlong evangelistic world tour to find the doors closed to the pas-

---

*Many Pacific Islanders and Asians immigrated to New Zealand in the '70s and '80s.

torate in Richmond. He took a church in Pennsylvania, then discovered at age 48 he was losing sight in his right eye. The doctor said it was stress and prescribed brisk walking—three miles a day. His daily route took him past a travel agency where a poster softly beckoned, "Come. See New Zealand."

He remembered well the morning he opened the door, saying, "Mother, you'd better pack. We're going to New Zealand." Within days the Pennsylvania church accepted Dad's resignation to follow God's call, and our family of three headed to California. The love offering from a revival plus liquidating their new car were enough to provide fare for the ship's passage. Personal belongings were placed in storage or sold. By the departure date, Dad's older children were either in college or married.* Dad felt free to go.

"But freedom doesn't always feel secure," he decided 34,000 feet above the ocean on his way to General Assembly. "Sometimes it's like being carried on the wind."

---

*Dad, a widower at age 36, had five of his six children with his first wife who died at 34 of pneumonia.

2

A Church Is in the Wind

I don't know what this seven-year-old did during those long nine weeks until Dad returned. I was not yet in public school, and Mother was too ill to tutor me. I have two memories of that time: one sad, one happy. I crept into Mother's room one day, feeling so lonely. I just needed to talk to someone. I leaned on the bed to see if she was awake. She was so sick she could not stand the bed to be jarred, even by a touch.

But one morning the sun shone; the sky was blue. Birds were singing ecstatic songs, begging the skeleton trees to come to life. The tree outside Mother's window responded with an explosion of pink. Mother also opted for life. Health returned, color was restored, and life again was filled with promise.

○ ○ ○

Mother was packing for our return to the United States when the cablegram arrived with the news. Permission had been granted to officially begin the work of the Church of the Nazarene in the land we already deeply loved. But how much work my parents could not have dreamed. They were filled with excitement but also with a great sense of responsibility.

The area from Balmoral to Mount Eden was central for the spreading city of Auckland, so that was where the search for church property began. To save time, Dad went one direction; Mother, another. Dad found a house in a residential neighborhood that was available and could be renovated into a meeting place. He was convinced this was the place the church should purchase. Mother was just as convinced it wasn't. Whenever she was that adamant, Dad listened. Within days we looked at a property on Dominion Road, one of the main arteries of the city. The brick house, numbered 675, had a basement room and garage that could be remodeled to serve as a chapel. And miracle of miracles, a bare corner lot was available right next door. Both were convinced—this must be the place God had in mind.

There was one problem. The house and corner lot were separate properties, belonging to different owners. The Griffiths, like Gideon of the Bible, put out a fleece: they would not take either property unless they could get both. They made offers, and both owners accepted within the hour.* The property at 675 Dominion Road was the Lord's to be cared for by the Church of the Nazarene. What a relief to have a home and a place for a church home.

---

*Richard S. Taylor, *Our Pacific Outposts* (Kansas City: Beacon Hill Press, 1956), 128.

The first parsonage at 675 Dominion Road

2001. I'm sitting in the office of Vipul Kharat, eight years the pastor of the church at Dominion Road. After the initial introductions, he says, "Perhaps the most far-reaching thing your parents did was to buy this property for the first church. For a small denomination to have this kind of visibility on a main viaduct of Auckland where thousands pass every day is invaluable."

Did I say that the corner lot was bare? Well, not quite! It had been a city dump for 30 years, and the rubbish was now camouflaged with eight-foot weeds. While waiting for legal possession of the land and home, Mother and Dad rented an old, nearly defunct Methodist church in the downtown area and conducted their first campaign under the Nazarene banner. As they looked out over the congregation that first night, they prayed, "Lord, give us a nucleus of people out of this group from which to begin the church." The Davises, the Tafts, and a godly, elderly man named Mr. Wilson attended the services and became solid charter members of the first Church of the Nazarene in New Zealand.

Daylight hours found Dad transforming the basement floor of our house into what we affectionately called the "Catacomb Chapel." Mother used her time to visit every house in the surrounding neighborhoods. She introduced herself, our church and services, and, when allowed, Jesus.

On January 1, 1953, we celebrated God's goodness and plan with an all-night prayer meeting in the newly completed chapel. The room seated about 60 and became the church home for the people God was sending our way. Mother held children's meetings after school where she kept the boys and girls spellbound by her wonderful flannelgraph stories.

2001. I knocked on the front door of the Dominion Road parsonage. This place had been my home from age 8 to 18. It was the same door, the same glass. But now by the door lay an assortment of worn sandals, 10 to 15 pairs. Pastor Vipul, born to a Nazarene pastor's family in India, opened the door and welcomed me. "Come in! Feel free to look around."

My eyes dropped to the floor where I was standing. This is where I sat listening through the crack in the door to Dad teaching the preachers' class. There were three in that first class: Jervis

The first preacher's class. (l. to r.) Phil Burton, Jervis Davis, and Ray Parker, circa 1950s.

(Jeff) Davis, Ray Parker, and Phil Burton. God was building pastors; later, they helped build the church.

General Superintendent G. B. Williamson visited New Zealand in March of 1953 and held a four-day preaching mission. His vision inspired the little band of people. He predicted a great harvest and challenged the people to build on the lot next to the parsonage. He shared with them Dad's dream of a building that would hold two to three hundred persons with a basement for Sunday School rooms.

Before the end of March, the people began the monumental task of clearing the lot of 30 years of city refuse! First they burned everything that would burn, and then carried off 14 Mack-size trucks of debris. As the last load was driven away, the little band of people became excited. Now the digging of the foundation could finally begin.

○ ○ ○

The "rock" conclusion was correct, but the inference in the word "just" was a gross underestimation.

○ ○ ○

Dad lifted his shovel and threw his weight into sinking the blade deep into the earth. Thud! His body was jarred by the impact. *It's just a rock*, he thought. The "rock" conclusion was correct, but the inference in the word "just" was a gross underestimation.

Dad took an iron stake and probed the soil in different places. Each examination brought the same result. "Surely not! It can't be!" But it was true. The entire section of land sat on a gigantic stratum of volcanic rock. If Dad were to build the church he envisioned, he would have to break through 10 to 12 feet of solid rock. What the church people thought would take weeks would require months of backbreaking labor.

"Lord, I guess you wanted this church to be built on solid rock literally as well as spiritually," Dad prayed. "Jesus, Cornerstone of our salvation, give me strength for the work."

For nine months, mostly alone, Dad worked with small amounts of dynamite and large amounts

The first shovel of cement for the church foundation

of sledgehammering and sweat, prying huge boulders with crowbars until the area was large enough for the prospective basement.

While Dad worked with rock and mortar, Mother worked with radio waves. She was invited to produce a weekly program on the government-owned station, lZB. Her broadcast title was "The Lady Traveler." One avid listener remembers, "The airtime was smack in the middle of the morning 'soaps,' so there was a tremendous audience, and the Lady Traveler became very well known." Another noted, "The mailing list alone was over 2,000. The program continued for three years and lent credibility to the unknown Church of the Nazarene."

After months of site preparation, we celebrated

by raising a large donated tent on the site and holding services.

In November 1953 the churchmen poured the foundation. George Yearbury was the contractor; Jack West, his foreman. Men and women in the church also came and worked whenever possible. These people were the "rocks" that God used to build His church in New Zealand. Allow me the privilege of introducing you to a few of them.

○ ○ ○

Jervis Davis was like an elder brother to me, always kind, with eyes that twinkled as if he knew a joyous secret. He is not a big man but can preach like a bishop. I loved his Georgian accent, especially when he sang, "This world is not my home; / I'm just a passing through." He was Dad's right-hand man.

2001. Jervis and I reminisced about the days when our families first met.

"I first met Rev. Griffith early in 1951," Jervis said. "He was touring the country with speaking engagements. One night I happened to be at an Auckland Youth for Christ rally where he was speaking. It was good to hear an American accent. After the service I introduced myself. He wondered what this Georgia boy was doing so far from home."

Jervis's story was not uncommon in times of war. While a Marine stationed in New Zealand, he met and married Maisie and settled in Auckland. Dad and Jervis visited a little and said good-bye, but it would not be the last time they would meet. Months later God put them together again.

Jervis Davis, 2001

"That day," Jervis said, "Rev. Griffith told me he wanted to go back to the States to ask the church leaders in Kansas City to commission him to open the Church of the Nazarene in New Zealand." They exchanged addresses and parted.

Jeff, as Dad nicknamed him (after Jefferson Davis), went to his own pastor to ask what he knew about Nazarenes. "They are good strong evangelicals," the minister replied. "Their work stands." While still in the United States, Jeff had prepared for the ministry. His long-range plan was to return to the States for more training, then he and his wife would go as missionaries to China. But God had a different field in mind.

"Rev. Griffith returned from the States," Jervis continued, "and invited us to come to the services they were holding in an old Methodist church. There we heard the message of holiness and began to long for this infilling of God's Holy Spirit.

"In the meantime Maisie and I were praying and seeking God's will for our lives. After three months we believed we had the answer. God wanted us to stay in New Zealand and help build His Church through the Church of the Nazarene."

And build they did. They pioneered the church in Hamilton, pastored Kerr's Road and Breezes Road in Christchurch, and in 1975 pioneered another church in Bishopdale.

Maisie, his partner in every way, died in 1997. Jervis has faithfully continued to serve as pastor, and in 2001 celebrated 48 years of service to God. The lives that have been touched through his obedience have gone out to touch others in beautiful sequence and like ripples on the water keep growing and going.

○ ○ ○

Called Unto Holiness.
You are invited to attend a meeting where the way of scriptural holiness will be explained.

This newspaper ad drew the Taft family to the services in the old Bright Street Methodist Church in Auckland. They came with hungry hearts. From the very first service they were faithful. When the Catacomb Chapel was completed, they would get all four children washed and groomed, then travel two hours one way by bus from Point Chevalier to Dominion Road twice on Sunday and any other time the doors were opened. They never seemed to find it too much trouble. Aline had made a public confession of faith years before, but had always felt there was something more. The "more" came after hearing a message by G. B. Williamson on entire sanctification.

Her daughter Annette Taft Brown fills in the story. "There was a great struggle within Mum to take this step of faith. Giving herself totally to the Lord was not so difficult, but she felt God was also asking her to commit to this tiny 'unknown' church. Her entire family were staunch members of an established, respected denomination. Her father was an elder, a lifelong position. It was an emotionally wrenching decision to go against the tide of her beloved family to become a part of what they considered a fly-by-night and possibly even spiritually dangerous sect.

"Mum struggled for four days before surrendering everything to the Lord. She did not sense any cataclysmic change, but she testified, 'The next day the realization swept over me that the Holy Spirit had come. It was the turning point of my spiritual life.'"

But now, a significant question burned in Mrs. Taft's heart. She broached the subject with her new

The Taft family, circa 1950s

pastor. "Will this church be staying here permanently, and, if so, can we be a part of it?"

"We've been praying that someone would ask that question," Rev. Griffith responded.

With that confirmation, both the New Zealanders and expatriates moved forward with resolve, believing this church was God's plan and He would build it. In May 1953 the church was officially organized with 16 charter members, 11 adults and 5 children. The Tafts, Davises, and Mr. Wilson were among those who joined.

That day is crystal clear in Annette's memory. "I was eight years old, but the messages were clear and understandable. Rev. Griffith asked who would come forward to join the Church of the Nazarene. I didn't ask my parents; I just went to the front. This was my church, and I wanted to officially belong."

○ ○ ○

Aline Taft was the proverbial "church pillar" for 45 years.

○ ○ ○

"Dad, Mum, can I join the church also?" David Taft was only six years old. His parents questioned him regarding his personal knowledge of Jesus as Savior. When his answers showed that he understood, they agreed to ask Rev. Griffith, who responded with a quote from Isaiah, "A little child shall lead them." David also became a charter member.

Aline Taft was the proverbial "church pillar" for 45 years, holding key roles in the church locally and on the district until her home-going. Three of the six Taft children attended Australian Nazarene Bible College (now Nazarene Theological College). Judith married a pastor in Australia, and they have been ministering in that country ever since. David became a pastor and served in that capacity for many years. The youngest two girls have remained faithful to the Lord and His Church. (Annette's story appears in a later chapter.)

○ ○ ○

"Why is God so cruel?" Joan's question was to no one in particular and certainly not to God. She had stopped communicating with Him quite awhile before. At age 15 in her hometown of Hartlepool, England, she had found the Lord as her Savior under the ministry of Rev. E. Chapman of the International

Holiness Mission. But in 1948 she joined the British Army, and God was soon left far behind. She became engaged, and the wedding was planned for the day her army commitment was fulfilled. Then tragedy struck. Two weeks before the ceremony her fiancé was killed. Joan was devastated and the God question/accusation pounded its way relentlessly into her soul: "Why? How could God be so cruel?"

"I was heartbroken and lost, just wanting to get away—away from the pain and memories," Joan confesses. "In 1952 I decided to join the New Zealand Women's Royal Air Corps, enlisting in England. When I arrived in Wellington, I was ready to start a new life and live it up!

"Unknown to me, a missionary friend of Rev. Chapman knew of my spiritual condition and learned that a Church of the Nazarene was to be established in New Zealand. That woman contacted Rev. Chapman who in turn contacted Rev. Griffith.

"Wellington, located in the southern part of the North Island, was a 12-hour drive from Auckland. When Mr. Griffith received Rev. Chapman's letter, he had already planned a trip to Christchurch in the South Island to scope out the possibility of starting a church there. He stopped in Wellington, contacted Army Headquarters, and asked for me.

"Around Christmas in 1952 I had some leave time and was able to spend a few days with the Griffiths. They were praying I would be stationed in Auckland. I didn't believe it possible, but a couple of months later a miracle took place—I was transferred to Papakura near Auckland. I came back to the Lord and, oh, how my life changed! Twice a week I rode my bike to church services 35 kilometers (23 miles) each way.

○　○　○

How dare anyone call the story of God's love "bunkum"?

○　○　○

"The church at that time was being held in the parsonage basement on Dominion Road. I was a part of the group who cleared away the rubbish from the next-door lot. The work was backbreaking, but I didn't care. It was such a privilege to be part of the family of God.

"In 1955 I met Frank who was also in the Army. I want you . . . No, you *must* meet Frank!"

○　○　○

"Do you really believe this 'bunkum'?" The challenge was made to my father. The challenger was Frank Ranger. I was in the kitchen with them at the time and held my breath. How dare anyone call the story of God's love "bunkum"?

Frank is a "fair dinkum Kiwi." He says it the way he sees it and would never be caught dead "putting on airs." He's an incurable tease and can find humor in everything. He and his "Pommie" wife, as he affectionately calls her, planted four churches from 1972 to 1980 and assisted in planting a fifth. Together they have invested 106 years in the Church Jesus died for.

I shake my head in wonder at our God who transforms and makes usable some of us who are highly unlikely candidates. What is the key to this metamorphosis? I believe it's the amazing grace of God working in the willing heart of one who is totally surrendered to Him.

Yes, this is the man who called the tenets of the Christian faith "bunkum" after nine weeks of church attendance. But then, his goal was Joan, not God. By his own admission, the only reason he came to church was because Joan refused to go out with him unless he did.

When Frank had been attending for a month, saintly old Mr. Wilson approached him after the service. "Young man, you look bored." It was not an accusation, only an observation.

"Yes, I am." Frank's voice had a so-what intonation. "I only come because I'm coerced by that young woman over there."

"Do you listen?"

"No! I can't be bothered!" This also was said with no intention of softening the truth.

"Frank, will you do me a favor?"

Frank, wishing the elderly man would just leave him alone, said, "Uh . . . oh, well. . . . OK." His tone bordered on belligerence.

"Will you listen for three weeks?"

Knowing the habits of that godly man, I'm sure Frank was bathed in prayer the entire three weeks. At church his greetings were friendly, but he never mentioned their agreement. When the three weeks were over, Frank sat in the back of the chapel planning a quick escape. He had spotted Mr. Wilson on the front row, so knew he could make it out the door without confrontation.

Suddenly Mr. Wilson was between him and the door. (For 50 years, Frank has wondered how a man in his 80s could have moved that fast.)

"Frank, did you listen?" The question was kind but firm.

"Yes." Frank didn't expand on his one-syllable answer.

"Did you realize what was happening?" It was Mr. Wilson's only probe. Again the answer was yes.

"Well," said Mr. Wilson, and there was no mistaking the gratification in his voice. "You have a good day!"

The "bunkum" question did not erupt for two more weeks in our kitchen. I watched my father sift through the irreverent words to the seeking heart beneath. "Bunkum? No! Do I believe in Jesus and His Word? Absolutely! He's my very life and will be till God calls me home."

There was a pause as each man looked into the soul of the other. "Frank, can we pray together?"

Frank's silence was the only assent the pastor needed. Dad prayed that Frank would turn from his own way of living and receive the life Christ was offering him. When he finished, Frank responded, "Amen." He was agreeing with the prayer by stating, "So be it."

I remember wondering if this conversion was real. How could someone become a Christian just by saying amen? But time has proven the transaction between Frank and God was real. Frank began to attend the course for preachers, since it was a good place to learn more about Jesus. No one ever guessed Frank would become "one of them." God knew differently.

The "fair dinkum Kiwi" married the "Pommie" girl four months after he gave his life to Christ, and in 2003 it will be 50 years. According to Frank, Joan is a better preacher than he, and God has given them some wonderful adventures in serving Him. I think his exact words were, "We wouldn't trade the life God has given us for all the tea in China." Quite a statement for a Kiwi.

○ ○ ○

Jervis was smiling now, his thoughts dappled with memories.

○ ○ ○

2001. Jervis Davis and I are reminiscing again.

"Jervis, when did Phil Burton come to us?"

"Remember the tent campaign your folks held on the cleared property at Dominion Road? I walked in one night, and Phil Burton was leading the singing." (Phil had a booming voice and never did anything halfway). "I said to Griffith, 'Where did you get this guy?'"

Jervis was smiling now, his thoughts dappled with memories. I knew some of what he was thinking, for I had watched as these two men worked on the church building and like the cement they mixed, the friendship was solid through the years.

Phil Burton was another young man who wanted to love and serve God with all his heart. He had traveled to Australia to attend a Bible Training Institute (BTI) and there met a soft-spoken Aussie girl. Coed student relationships were taboo, so Phil and Beryl were careful not to pursue the relationship overtly until he returned to New Zealand.

"Soon after Phil went home," Beryl says, "a childhood friend Ray Parker invited him to visit the new church fellowship on Dominion Road. Phil declined the invitation. One Sunday he woke up too late to make it into town and decided to pop in and hear this Nazarene pastor. Phil's heart was drawn to the people and their message, but since he had never heard of this denomination, he thought he'd better check out their validity. His research was answered with 'They are good people and solid evangelicals.'

"The second positive in the Nazarene's favor was that students at BTI were required to have practical experience in building the Kingdom as well as Bible knowledge. When Phil discovered that Rev. Griffith was beginning a training class with doctrinal studies and opportunities for preaching and evangelism, he committed to join the Nazarenes."

But what about Beryl, his Aussie sweetheart of another doctrinal persuasion? Phil put her in touch with people at Australasian Nazarene Bible College who explained the meaning of the life of holiness. Before long she completely embraced "Phil's church"

Beryl Burton, 2001

and was ready to join him in whatever God had in mind for them to do.

Phil was the other right-hand man in the beginning years and pioneered the third church on the district. Rev. and Mrs. Burton faithfully invested their lives in the New Zealand church until Phil died in 1991. Beryl continues to serve wherever God gives her opportunity.

○ ○ ○

The sound of shattering glass reverberated down

the quiet street. A man had deliberately thrown his keys through the glass in his front door. Was he angry or drunk? No, it seemed more like a ceremony than a thoughtless act. There was a racehorse beautifully etched in the glass, but now only a jagged hole. For this man named Maurice Thomas, this was symbolic of a new direction, new priorities, new life. The hole would be filled with God himself. No longer would he allow anything to come between his relationship with His Savior and Lord. The only race he was now passionate about winning was the one the writer of Hebrews wrote about in chapter 12, verses 1-2.

○ ○ ○

There was a racehorse beautifully etched in the glass, but now only a jagged hole.

○ ○ ○

Why the change? Was it overnight? No, it began months before on the day Mother's visitation route included Marsden Avenue. She found a lady sitting on her veranda soaking in the weak warmth of the winter sun, recuperating from tuberculosis. Her name was June Thomas. Mother invited her to church, and both she and her husband, Maurice, came with Judy and Pam, their two little girls. They came once, twice, and just kept coming.

June had become a Christian during her illness when in desperation she had gone to an Elim House of Prayer. There people prayed for her and told her how to know Jesus—the Way, the Truth, and the

Life. Her own kitchen became a holy place; for there she opened her heart to Christ's saving love.

Maurice had seen the transformation in his wife and had clearly heard the gospel but was not ready to give up his racehorses. "One Sunday night after church, the Griffiths invited us over for supper," he says. "In his direct way, Griffy said, 'Maurice, why aren't you a Christian?' We talked awhile, and before we went home I prayed to become a new creation in Christ Jesus.

"We kept going to the church, and I became established in the faith under the Griffiths' ministry. Eventually I sold my bakery business. Rev. Griffith needed a hand with the building, and I pitched in to help. The pay was about 10 pounds (U.S.$30) a week, so we had to supplement with our savings."

June picks up their story. "Finances became

Maurice and June Thomas with Connie (center), 2001

tighter and tighter until at Christmas there was no money for gifts, but somehow the Lord helped us to make it. One night at a Christian Endeavor meeting we were called into full-time service with Christian Literature Crusade (CLC). During our training in Australia we joined the Church of the Nazarene and never moved our membership."

The Thomases worked with CLC for 20 years: in Papua New Guinea, the Philippines, and as field leader from the home base in New Zealand. Their lives have been exemplary and a joy to all who know them. Like Paul the apostle, the Thomases will be able to say, "I have fought the good fight, I have finished the race, I have kept the faith" (2 Tim. 4:7).

3

Like Ripples on the Water

One Christmas very few presents were under the tree. To make the skimpy Christmas more exciting, Mother rigged an indoor treasure hunt. When I read the final clue and discovered the "treasure," I could hardly hide my disappointment. The box fit inside my hand. There couldn't be anything of importance inside something so small.

I opened it slowly, partly because it was the last present and partly to shield my hopes from further dashing. Removing the lid, I pulled back the tiny piece of cotton. For the next split second I was stunned into silence and then exploded with a squeal. The watch I had longed to own for two years lay in my hand. I felt I would burst with gratitude and joy.

As I wrote this chapter, I felt some of those same emotions. Although the New Zealand District is not large and none of her churches has achieved megachurch status, her contributions to the Kingdom have been of a magnitude that belies her size.

Like ripples caused by dropping pebbles on water, the effects of God working in and through self-surrendered lives have moved outward, farther outward, and still farther outward to impact Europe, Papua New Guinea, the Samoan Islands, Australia, Vietnam, the United States, the Philippines, and Bangladesh. Only eternity will tell the whole story. But may I trace for you a few of the "ripples"?

Neville Bartle—Papua New Guinea and Fiji

2001. I'm standing in the basement fellowship hall of the Dominion Road Church. My eyes glisten with tears as they follow the lines of the concrete block walls. These are the walls my father and the men in the church laid nearly 50 years ago. I cannot quite grasp the reality that God has made it

Dominion Road Church, 1958

possible for me to be here in New Zealand in time for this event. Upstairs in the sanctuary, a memorial service for Ollie Bartle, patriarch of the New Zealand church, has just concluded. Ollie went to be with his Lord four days before I arrived, and his sons, whom I knew from district youth camps, have flown in from all over the world. It was a moving experience as son after son and friend after friend told of the qualities of this unpretentious saint and the impact of his life and prayers.

My reflection is interrupted by a touch on the elbow and the voice of Neville Bartle. "If it weren't for your parents, I wouldn't be here." I smile in gratitude at the tribute and greet him. I knew the "here" in his statement did not refer to the church we were standing in or the occasion but to the

Neville Bartle

The Bartle family, 2001. Neville is fourth from the right.

places God has taken and used him as His ambassador for 32 years in Papua New Guinea and now, more recently, the Fiji Islands.

Neville is in great part the product of a devout Christian father and mother. To me, he was just one of the Bartle boys, but even as a young boy he was serious about the things of God. As a teen and young adult, he was active in the ministry of the church wherever he was. In university Neville trained to be a lab technician, and the next thing we knew he was in Papua New Guinea (PNG), working in the Nazarene Mission Hospital at Kudjip.

The World Mission Department recognized Neville's talents and heart for the Lord and commissioned him as full-time career missionary in 1970.

He is known throughout PNG for his picture sermons. With a large population of the country being preliterate, he developed a way to teach God's Word through stick figures drawn on a flip chart. Bible college students help to silk screen the charts and go out to teach people in the most remote areas of that land. From the "back of beyond" in the Western Highlands Province, to the malaria-infested Sepik River valleys, the lessons of Jesus have been and are being taught to thousands of people.

While on furlough one year Neville earned a master's degree at Fuller Theological Seminary in California. I always wondered who learned more, Neville or his professors? More recently, Neville has earned his doctorate in missiology from Asbury Theological Seminary, and he and Joyce have taken an assignment in the Fiji Islands where he is coordinating theological education for the South Pacific Field.

And the ripples move ever outward.

Annette Taft Brown—Samoa, United States

Just three of us girls grew up in the Dominion Road Church—the Taft girls and me. We were eight and nine years of age when we all became charter members. Judith was a little older and much wiser than I; Annette, a little younger but always smarter.

Judith and Annette were a steadying influence on my life. No matter how "different" I felt at school during the week, at church I was OK. We were Nazarenes together. From second graders playing dolls or acting out fairy tales, to teenagers buffing our nails, and to the present time, we have been friends.

Annette finished Auckland Girls Grammar (high) School, and after working for four years had earned enough to attend Australasian Nazarene Bible College. She felt called to be a minister of the gospel, and upon graduation returned to New Zealand to pastor the New Lynn church in Auckland. The young church flourished under Annette's shepherding for seven years. Feeling the need for more education, she enrolled in Nazarene Theological Seminary in Kansas City.

In the late 1970s she went as a missionary to Samoa, a New Zealand protectorate. There were only five churches at that time. Annette pastored one of them and taught at the Bible college.

One day, an older student named Mika came to her. "Miss Annette, there's a new family up the road. They're building a house, and we need to welcome them."

"Good idea, Mika. How should we do it?"

"We should make up a food basket and take it to them." Mika understood how hungry you get building a house.

○   ○   ○

A basket of food coupled with the political position of our Samoan brother, and the Lord was able to accomplish the "impossible."

○   ○   ○

Annette and Mika gathered the things Samoans

like to eat, made up an attractive basket, and took it to the hard-working family. The man worked for the United Nations (UN). Through this small act of kindness, he and his family came to the church desiring to know the Jesus these people served. Although Annette returned to the United States two weeks after she met them, they were discipled by studying God's Word and observing the lives of other Christians.

Sometime later this UN official was assigned to Bangladesh. While there he did the same thing the Christians did in Samoa, he invited people to study the Bible. As they studied they received the truth, and the way was opened for the Church of the Nazarene to begin a compassionate ministry. Since Bangladesh is not an easy-access country, ordinary methods would not have worked. God needed a certain vessel to reach those precious people. A basket of food coupled with the political position of our Samoan brother, and the Lord was able to accomplish the "impossible."

His next assignment was in Southeast Asia. Again he began Bible studies where the people grew in faith and the numbers multiplied. He hung a sign outside of the building where they met. The sign read "Church of the Nazarene."

So does the sign in front of the San Bruno Church in northern California pastored by Steve and Annette Brown. Together they shepherd a multicultural church. In 2000 Annette was asked to speak at the first International All Samoan Nazarene Conference. Annette is also involved in theological education for pastors from Asia and the South Pacific who are ministering in the San Francisco Bay area.

And the ripples move ever outward.

Nick and Beverly Faataape—Samoa, Australia

The Richard Greens, devoted Salvation Army laypeople, became fast friends with our family from the moment we met. Many times they invited us to their beautiful place in the Canterbury Plains of the South Island. They supported and encouraged my folks in many ways. Rich Green had a successful bakery in Christchurch where one could eat the best scones and cream cakes known to man or woman.

Beverly, their daughter, fills us in on her story. "By the time I reached my early 20s, God no longer took first place in my life. I married a young man from Samoa who later became a chief. The first years of our marriage were very unstable; Nikolao was not a Christian. But during this time I recommitted my life to Christ."

Bev also turned to the pastors of the church in Christchurch, Jervis and Maisie Davis. They counseled and prayed together. This support continued even when the young couple moved with their family to Samoa. A year after being back in his own land, Nikolao gave his heart to the Lord. All who knew them began to see the reality when they sang the old song, "What a wonderful change in my life has been wrought / Since Jesus came into my heart!"

Today, Nick and Bev pastor a church in Australia that ministers especially to immigrated Samoans. The people see the grace of God working in the Faataapes' lives and desire to also know His life-giving, life-changing power.

And the ripples spread ever outward.

Jeanine van Beek—Holland, Germany, Haiti

Jeanine's father was Dutch and in the tulip business. Her French mother was a high-fashion Parisian model. Her father, scarred and disillusioned by war, longed to live in a quiet place as far away from the memories as possible. From the Netherlands they chose the peaceful city of Christchurch, New Zealand. Here in "the garden city" our paths crossed.

With reinforcements from the States in the persons of the H. S. Palmquists, our family was free to leave Auckland and pioneer the work on the South Island. Christchurch, the largest city, was the logical choice. As always, Dad contacted church leaders and Christian organizations in the area to introduce our church and purpose. John Beaumont was the head of Youth for Christ at that time.

Jeanine worked with the YMCA. When Corrie ten Boom came to New Zealand on a speaking tour, Jeanine, because of their common language, was asked to be her companion. At that time Jeanine became acquainted with John and his wife. One day while they were discussing spiritual matters and in particular a deeper walk with the Lord, John said, "You ought to meet the people called Nazarenes." He put Jeanine in touch with my parents.

Around that time Richard S. Taylor, then director of the Australasian Nazarene Bible College (ANBC), came for a week of services. He proclaimed clearly the doctrine of holiness to our embryo congregation. Jeanine listened carefully, analytically, and wanted to learn more of this life that could be cleansed and set apart to live wholly for God.

Within weeks she and four others were on their way to Australia to enroll in the Nazarene Bible College. Jeanine graduated and went on to Northwest Nazarene College (now University) to finish her bachelor's degree, and then to Colorado State University and Southern Nazarene University to receive a master's degree. Returning to Europe to pastor a church in Germany, she accepted the invitation of some old friends to meet and share with Cor and Miep Holleman regarding what the apostle Paul termed "the more excellent way." This core group was the catalyst for the founding of the Church of the Nazarene in the Netherlands.

Soon after Jeanine went to teach and work at the newly founded European Nazarene Bible College (ENBC) in Büsingen, Germany. Along with being a gifted teacher, she was indispensable as a translator in the early days of that institution. With students from many nations, Jeanine's ability to speak five languages fluently was a major asset.

After nine years in Büsingen she was asked to go to Haiti to direct the Bible college there. Hundreds of pastors were trained during the 15 years of her leadership. When her health forced her to make a change, she was asked to return to ENBC (now European Nazarene College) as rector and held this position for eight years. In April 1999 she immigrated to the United States and continued teaching and preaching in Haiti and the French Antilles until she retired. Today there are countless missionaries and pastors worldwide who have been influenced by this dedicated woman.

And the ripples move ever outward.

Work and Witness Teams—Papua New Guinea and Fiji

New Zealand has sent Work and Witness teams to both Papua New Guinea and the Fiji Islands. Bob and Maureen Gordon and Bharat and Dorothy Bhanabais are only four of an enthusiastic group of New Zealanders who have been involved in these God-blessed outreaches.

2001. I sat with Bob and Maureen and watched videos of two New Zealand Work and Witness trips to Papua New Guinea. I could sense the joy they feel at being participants of such an adventure for God.

○ ○ ○

Thirty-two team members! I can remember when there were not that many Nazarenes in all of New Zealand!

○ ○ ○

"They were led," Bob told me, "by Glenn Stott in cooperation with Neville Bartle. Six New Zealand churches were represented on each trip. The first time we built a parsonage in Mendi in seven days.

Three years later our project was a small church in the same town. The three-ply laminated beams were built on site with thousands of nails and many hammers wielded by our 32-member team."

I'm thinking, *Thirty-two team members! I can remember when there were not that many Nazarenes in all of New Zealand!*

"The beams were raised with ropes," Bob continued, "and pushed into place with poles by a large crowd of the local people working with our team. We [the New Zealand District] will send another W&W team soon. This time it will be a medical trip to Fiji."

His pride in what God has done is well-founded.

For the ripples move ever outward.

○ ○ ○

Dorothy Bhanabais and her husband, Bharat, are attorneys with East Indian and Fijian family roots. They are active in working with disadvantaged immigrants and serve in the All Nations Church of the Nazarene. Since Dorothy coordinated the medical Work and Witness trip to Fiji, I asked her to evaluate the effectiveness of their efforts.

"The Work and Witness trip to Fiji was truly blessed by the Lord," Dorothy said. "Approximately 300 people passed through the clinic that week. Our health professionals commented that it was the most satisfying work they've ever done in their lives. We were well received by the locals and the officials. The secretary for the Ministry of Health wrote conveying appreciation and indicated they would be pleased for us to do other similar missions. We're waiting God's leading on this and believe we'll repeat minimissions of this nature in the future. A man from a nearby village offered land for the Church of the Nazarene to build a clinic and a church building. We praise our wonderful Lord and Savior for His equipping and enabling. He is so faithful. All we need do is obey and trust."

And the ripples embrace the next generation.

Susie Bartle—Bangladesh

Susie Bartle is the daughter of Neville and Joyce Bartle. Together with her siblings and parents, she has lived nearly all her life on the mission field. This experience, blended with the role-modeling of her parents and other missionaries, developed within her a deep desire to help those with so little to know Jesus—abundantly.

○ ○ ○

God gives us the desires of our hearts and then empowers the fulfillment of the dream.

○ ○ ○

Susie graduated from high school in Papua New Guinea in 1992 and left home to be with her elder sister, Kathryn, in New Zealand. She received teacher training at Auckland College of Education and Auckland University. In 1995 Susie served for a year as a volunteer back home in Papua New Guinea, involved in children's ministries and the publication department. While in university she began teaching

English to a few refugees from Somalia. This experience developed a deep concern for Muslim women.

After graduation from university in 1997, she taught school for two and a half years in New Zealand. Then in August 2000 Susie went as a missionary to Bangladesh. Susie is teaching children from many different nationalities at Grace International School where about half of the children are missionary kids. God has equipped her for the task, for she relates easily with people different than herself and understands what it is to be a missionary kid. And the bonus? Bangladesh is 88.3 percent Muslim. When Susie is not in school, she reaches out to Muslim women. God gives us the desires of our hearts and then empowers the fulfillment of the dream. How wondrous is our God!

And the ripples . . .

Stephen Bennett—Philippines

John and Judy Bennett welcomed their first son, Stephen, in 1963. They taught him to love the Lord as he grew up in their Nazarene parsonages at Whangarei and Wainuiomata. In 1974 the family moved to Auckland and attended the New Lynn church where Annette Taft was pastor. Under her ministry Stephen consecrated himself completely to God.

As a teen Stephen was always active in the church, but when he was offered an opportunity to attend the Nazarene Youth Congress in Mexico, the zeal and determination of this young man was unveiled. To finance the trip he worked full-time all summer as a janitor in a sweets factory and part-time at the local Kentucky Fried Chicken. "The hard work was worth it," Stephen insists, "for the youth congress was an important spiritual experience where I was challenged not only to be a disciple of Jesus Christ but to make disciples."

While studying at Auckland University, Stephen was involved with a Christian student organization that, at times, gave mission presentations. The flame of his missions interest was fanned, and in the final year, he felt God's call to become a missionary. He wrote to the World Mission Department in Kansas City and in 1987 was accepted at Nazarene Theological Seminary (NTS) in Kansas City. Following the advice of missionary Neville Bartle, Stephen contacted World Mission about teaching in Papua New Guinea on a specialized assignment. Instead of PNG, the church appointed him to the Philippines.

Stephen took advantage of the college Christmas break to marry Christi-An Clifford, a former fellow NTS student. Together they have taught in six Nazarene colleges and pastored in three countries. In 2000, with qualifications completed, they went to the Philippines for a two-year missionary appointment to teach at Asia-Pacific Nazarene Theological Seminary. They are passing the baton, teaching others not only to be disciples of Christ but also to "go and make disciples of all nations, baptizing . . . and teaching them" (Matthew 28:19-20).

And the ripples will spread to eternity.

But today, we must catch the waves. Come, ride the waves with me.

4

Riding the Waves

Lifting the flap of the entrance to the tent, we gasped in unison as we surveyed the devastation. Benches were smashed or the legs broken, and the top of the tent, cut in strips with a knife, hung to the floor like streamers. It was autumn of 1954.

A group of us from the church was there to hold a tent mission on the far side of the city—out by the tomato farms in an area that was virtually untouched by evangelistic churches. The tent had been donated by Christian friends. Dad and some of his "preacher's class" had built the rough but adequate wooden benches. In the weeks leading up to the campaign, we had distributed a few hundred home-made flyers and covered the event with prayer.

The first two nights the attendance was small but otherwise uneventful. And now this! All of us looked at Dad to see what his response would be. The sadness in his face quickly changed to resolve. He squared his shoulders to match the set of his jaw. "Connie, would you get the hammer out of the car? Let's see if we can't make some of these benches work. Mother, do you think we could sew those strips back in place? No, not tonight. I'll find a ladder and throw the strips over the top temporarily."

The Griffiths in New Zealand, 1956

We finished all we could do to restore order, replaced the sign stating "Service Tonight," then stood in a circle and prayed. "Lord, we see the enemy doesn't like what we're doing here. But You have sent us here to proclaim Your good news. Help us as Joshua said to 'not to be terrified or discouraged,' but to go forward in the strength and power of Your Spirit." There was a hearty agreement of amens as we left the circle encouraged and took our places. But what would happen next? Was I the only one who felt a shiver in my spine?

○ ○ ○

The newspaper headlines screamed, "Otara—City Without a Soul." The year was 1974, and most of the predominately Polynesian population were newly emigrated from the quiet, peace-loving islands of Niue, Cook, Samoa, and Tonga. As is so often the case when young people are uprooted from simple cultural roots and moved to the impersonality of the modern city, they become lost in a sea of disconnection, and evil finds fertile ground. But God had a plan to place a beacon of hope in Otara and placed His hand on the hearts of Frank and Joan Ranger.

"We had returned from England in 1964," Joan said, "and once again continued to worship at the Dominion Road Church. But Frank and I felt led to start a work in Otara, a part of Auckland. We began in 1973, and Rev. Darrell Teare, the district superintendent, found a house for us on a street called Hope Place. Door-knocking commenced, plus lots of prayer, and before long a Sunday School* was being held in our home. Eventually the parents came along. Ollie and Evelyn Bartle moved to Otara and helped with the work. Souls were won for the Lord."

Neville Bartle writes of his parent's contribution in Otara. "They were there at the beginning, providing stability and role-modeling. They lived what it meant to be loyal, supportive laypeople and prayer warriors. Dad had a great desire to share the message of holiness and often invited people to their home. Over a cup of tea and biscuits he would talk to them of the necessity of living a holy life." Neville's mother, Evelyn, was the epitome of the astute church

---

*Traditionally Sunday School is only for children in New Zealand culture.

treasurer until the age 78. Ollie continued to take an active part in the church until age 86.

"The Lord added to the church," Joan Ranger says. "Worship services were moved to Bairds Intermediate School and then to the Presbyterian Church. From the beginning we saw miracle after miracle. It was our Pentecost. The church in Otara consists mainly of Islanders. There is, in fact, a mission field of Polynesian people within New Zealand. Before long Rev. Teare purchased property to have our own church built. The location—East Tamaki Road."

August 2001. I stared at the yellowed and stained paper I had just pulled out of an old box, long in storage. Scribbled there were three recipes given to my mother 50 years before by a woman in the church. I was busy deciphering the faded in-

Joan and Frank Ranger

structions until I saw that my oven could not perform as instructed. En route to the rubbish bin, I turned it over.

It took me a few seconds to comprehend what I was seeing. The recipes were written on the back of a flyer that advertised the infamous Tamaki tent meeting. I was incredulous to find this old paper with so many memories attached. But the line that excited me was the address: "corner of Hobson Dr. and Tripoli Rd., Tamaki."

While visiting New Zealand five months before, I tried to determine exactly where that tent meeting was held, because I believed the Otara church was located in the same vicinity. Here was the proof! "This church, I believe," I told the Otara congregation one Sunday morning, "is within blocks of that tent meeting. God raised up a witness in that day, and He is completing it in you. Nothing done for God in Jesus' name is ever wasted." The room resounded with praise to the Lord.

○ ○ ○

When Jesus said, "I will build my church," it was not just words idly thrown on the wind, but an indestructible covenant backed by the power and might of the omnipotent Creator.

○ ○ ○

When the property for the Otara church was purchased, none of them knew of the tent mission in Tamaki, but God knew. When Jesus said, "I will build my church," it was not just words idly thrown on the wind, but an indestructible covenant backed by the power and might of the omnipotent Creator.

○ ○ ○

The Pacific Islanders were not the only ones riding the waves.

"Michael's a fool! Why does he insist on going to church every Sunday? We could already be at the beach surfing if it wasn't for him." Glenn Stott was complaining to another 17-year-old as they waited impatiently for Michael to get home from church. Finally the delay became too much for them. "We drove to the New Lynn church, roared into the parking lot, banged the doors as loudly as possible as we entered the church, and sat down noisily on the back pew to wait. When the service was over, instead of everyone glaring at us, we were greeted warmly and invited to come back."

○ ○ ○

I could feel my face flush with excitement.

○ ○ ○

2001. Pastor Glenn is narrating his story as we sit around the Sunday dinner table.

"We were so blown away that they seemed to want us we kept going back. Annette Taft was the pastor then. She encouraged all of us young people to attend the Camp at Piha. That was where I gave my heart to the Lord. But the next year I was back and forth, trying to hold on to the fun of the world and still have a little bit of God. Then the George Ronnekamps came. You know the Ronnekamps don't you? I think they had something to do with your folks coming to New Zealand. Anyway, I had no interest in them. George was . . . well, I just thought they were weird Americans.

"One day I was having a conversation with George's wife, Lois. She said, 'Jesus means a lot to you doesn't he, Glenn?' That simple question jolted me into thinking about what Jesus did mean to me and to focus my attention on what was really important.

"The next Sunday George was sick, and Lois preached. In the middle of the sermon I remember saying to myself, 'If she doesn't stop talking, I'm going to have to interrupt the service to go pray at the altar.'"

"Excuse me, Glenn. Is this Ronnekamp the ex-Marine who told my father he should go to New Zealand? Do you mean that years later he came— himself?" I could feel my face flush with excitement. Oh, how awesome our God is! "Glenn, do you know where these people are? Can you tell me how to contact them?"

By the next morning, Glenn had contacted Ronnekamps and before long, ties almost forgotten had been renewed.

Lois E-mailed their story. "In 1977 Dr. Jerald Johnson contacted George and me about a two-year stint of pastoring either in Australia or New Zealand. We were amazed because George had never expressed to anyone the desire to go there. I had a difficult time with the call. My sister was dying of cancer, and our only grandchild was just two. To think of leaving George's aged mother and my father in his 90s was the hardest thing. But when I prayed, it was like the Lord said, 'I'll take care of them.' George phoned Dr. Johnson with an affirmative response. Our assignment would be New Lynn, a home mission church in Auckland. Our salary, $400 a month. A family friend Janet Houmes left a professorship at Tulsa University to come and help—at no salary.

"We soon discovered that most of the congregation were young teenagers. The Lord impressed upon George and me that if anything was accomplished for Him there would have to be much prayer. We were pressed for time. A two-year visa was all we were promised. We were pushing 60, and according to New Zealand law we were to be gone by then. Immediately, George announced there would be prayer at the church every day at noon, Monday through Friday, to pray for revival. Janet was always there with the two of us, and others would come as they were able. We would pray until we felt we had touched the Lord.

"That first week we also began having special times with the teens. Friday evenings George met with them in Janet's garage. There was Bible reading and prayer, and the teens would talk about their week. Hot tea and guava bars were always welcome, so I baked the bars, steeped the tea, and delivered it to the garage. This continued as long as we were there.

"A visitor from America once asked me if we were enjoying the beauty of the country. I said we surely did, what we had seen of it, but our goal was revival. We were hungry to see the Lord change the lives of these young people. The visitor, who had previously worked in New Zealand, said, 'People here are not particularly bent on religion.' The statement may have been true, but we refused to be daunted and kept praying and believing that the Lord was going to do something. Eight months later on August 13, 1978, God came. There are not words to describe that service. It was like a breeze sweeping from one side of the sanctuary to the other. Those precious teens, one by one came and knelt and prayed."

Glenn remembers, "I wasn't the only one that day who couldn't wait for Lois to stop preaching. Nearly all the people in the congregation went for-

Rev. and Mrs. Glenn Stott and daughters, 2001

ward to pray. Out of that group, five went to Bible college, and the ones who remained are faithful to this day."

"The Lord made it very clear to us," Lois says, "there were many lessons yet to be taught. The people must learn to be faithful in prayer and reading their Bibles. The entire second year was given to these important issues. One of this group is a teacher, another an attorney, Glenn Stott is a minister of the Word—and on it goes. We can only say, 'To God be the glory!'"

2001. "Glenn, do you believe that the wind of the Spirit still blows in New Zealand?"

"Absolutely! When we as individuals say a full and emphatic yes to His every leading and are available to do whatever He asks, whether it's running a Kid's Club, scrubbing a floor, visiting a neighbor, or transporting someone, He will use us."

5

The Wind Still Blows

2001. The energy in his step and the light in his smile belie the fact that Frank Kaio is older now. He's on a mission and must be quick about it. The city bus stops in front of his house and people are standing out there in the cold. He approaches the two or three waiting passengers and holds out cups of steaming, hot tea to them. In answer to their questioning eyes he simply says, "Because of Jesus." The words are steeped in loving purpose.

In earlier days Frank Kaio was a professional boxer. Part of his workout training was to run several miles daily. Often his route took him down Dominion Road, directly by the Church of the Nazarene, and every time his heart was convicted. He would say to himself, "There's the place I gave my life to God. A reasonable thing since He died for me. I promised to go God's way, but now . . ."

Looking back, Frank admits, "I felt so awful every time I passed the church, but it wasn't enough to make me change."

○ ○ ○

**The only casualties, however, were
the ketchup-spattered walls.**

○ ○ ○

As he ran he would sometimes allow himself to relive the events that took him to the church in the first place. "I was a member of the well-known Allen Gang, a sect of the Bodgies and Widgies cult of the '50s," he says. "Five or six of my gang were hanging with me on Great North Road when an old van stopped and a short, curly-haired man got out to ask if we would go to church with him. Church was not exactly on our agenda, but we always had time for food. And since the guy had mentioned a sausage feed, we climbed in."

They had no idea what they were in for. The church was having a special outreach in the basement every Friday for Bodgies (male) and Widgies (female). Singing, a gospel message, and food were the offered fare. One night members of opposing gangs came, and a food fight broke out. The only casualties, however, were the ketchup-spattered walls.

Frank returned to the church four times and during one of those meetings made the commitment to receive Jesus as his Savior.

But that was 17 years ago, he thought as he ran. *I was young and impressionable. It's too late to go back.*

He was married with two children before he would again talk to God.

Frank was pensive as he told the rest of the story, "Our two little ones became very ill, and I was desperate to help them. I went to my aunt, who I knew was a Christian, begging her to pray for God to heal them. She said, 'I'll pray but you need to turn from the direction you are going, give your whole life to God, and get in church so you can learn God's ways.'"

He knelt there in her living room and prayed. God received, as He always does, the repentant prodigal to be His reclaimed son.

"By the way, Auntie, what church do you attend?"

"The Church of the Nazarene," she answered.

2001. I look into the gentle eyes of this stately man. It has been 30 years since that scenario and Frank has never looked back.

In 1978 he joined the ministerial studies program and 12 years later was ordained. Since 1980 he has pastored the Papakura Church and consistently finds ways to love people, just "because of Jesus."

"Cup of hot tea, anyone?"

○ ○ ○

2001. I stare wide-eyed at the attractive lady across the table from me. "You don't mean it! I can't believe it!" I was interviewing the pastors of the Hamilton Church of the Nazarene over a cozy lunch. While getting acquainted, we discovered that the pastor's wife and I had already met 51 years before. The place: Belfast, Ireland, at a double birthday party—her ninth, my fifth. Rather stunned at another of God's surprises, I try to gather my thoughts and continue the interview. Joe and Naomi Tranter Bentham have recently returned to New Zealand from the British Isles South District after being away for 20 years. God has definitely led them back. But let's begin at the beginning.

The Benthams came as immigrants in September 1973. What had possessed them to leave their homeland with three children to live in the farthest-flung nation in the British Commonwealth? Here's their fascinating story.

○ ○ ○

Naomi welcomed the announcement, for it meant escape from family pressure to be involved in church.

○ ○ ○

Two years earlier, Naomi's aunt from New Zealand, had visited England. While showing her slides, God spoke to Joe, "I want you in New Zealand." Joe prayed for two years, waiting before the Lord. "When, God, when?" he asked over and over.

One day the Lord said, "Now, Joe!"

Naomi welcomed the announcement, for it meant escape from family pressure to be involved in church. But there was one problem with the planned exodus. They had just bought a new house and were told it would not sell.

Joe called a travel agent, "Can you find a five-berth passage to New Zealand?"

"Not this time of year."

"Well, give me a call if one comes up."

By the next day the travel agent had found for them a rather luxurious room. Naomi heard the phone ring and Joe's response, "I'll take it." Naomi shouted at him from the other room, "You'll take what? You're crazy! The house hasn't sold."

○ ○ ○

The congregation was singing "A New Name in Glory," and it rocked!

○ ○ ○

Joe hung up the phone, saying calmly, "It will sell."

There were 30 houses for sale in the neighborhood. A lady down the street had been trying to sell her house for two years. Within one week the Bentham house sold.

In Auckland, Joe was hired almost immediately as a business manager in a successful downtown enterprise. Just as quickly, Frank Ranger called and invited them to their church service in Otara. The first time they attended, Naomi was asked to play the piano. This was normal for her, but playing with guitar accompaniment was rather a shock for a musician of strict British upbringing. The congregation was singing "A New Name in Glory," and it rocked!

When they asked Joe to speak in the church, he hesitatingly consented. "But the day I preached, it just felt so right," he said. "When I finished, I sat down and began to pray, and the Lord whispered that this is the harvest field. "Lord, if you want me in full-time service, seal it with one seeker at the altar. I looked up, and the altar was lined. I knew why God had brought us to New Zealand."

Several rows away Naomi felt what was happening. "Lord," she said. "You wouldn't dare. You know I'm not in the place spiritually to be a pastor's wife."

A week later the children were singing "If That Isn't Love." Their faces were shining, and they sang with such feeling. It was like the Lord said to Naomi, "Those kids know Me with more reality than you ever have." She bowed her head and heart, confessed her sin of inner rebellion and hypocrisy, and surrendered her life to the Lordship of Christ.

"God had to make a lot of changes in me before I was fit to be a pastor's wife in a multicultural church," Naomi admits. "He showed me that no matter what my family or cultural background, at the cross of Jesus the ground is level."

Joe began ministerial studies with District Superintendent Darrell Teare, and from October 1974 to 1978 pastored the Otara church. When the church outgrew the rented Presbyterian Hall, the congregation purchased land. The Hamilton church called Joe to be their pastor, then after 18 months sent him to Australia to finish his studies to become a minister. He was ordained in 1981. In the meantime, a phone call came from New Zealand, saying there were no churches available for them to pastor. Deeply disappointed, Joe pastored churches in Australia and the United Kingdom until Naomi's health broke.

The doctor said they must get out of the ministry if Naomi were to live, for she could not bear to sit back and not be on the "front lines." (Was this the same lady who gladly left Britain so she wouldn't have to be involved in the church?) In response to the doctor's mandate, Joe became an enquiry officer with the police, and Naomi regained her health. In 1999, still in England, they received another phone call that would change their destiny. It was the Hamilton church, calling again after all those years. "Would they come and be their pastors?"

Joe was honest with them. "We can't possibly come until the year 2000. We have accrued a large debt and need time to pay for it. Also Naomi needs a hip replacement, and we must be in the United Kingdom for the health program to cover the expenses." The people in Hamilton said, "We'll wait, however long it takes."

Rev. Bentham was thrilled, but Naomi was struggling, for by now there were grandchildren. Their son begged, "Please don't tear the family up." Naomi went to her bedroom distraught. In the night she felt the Lord saying, "Naomi, give it up."

"What Lord?"

"Your family."

She surrendered her precious family into the capable and loving hands of her Heavenly Father. Within days a donor had given them 7.5 thousand pounds, enough to pay the debt. And Britain's medical system agreed to pay for the surgery—even if done in New Zealand. Six months later they were in New Zealand, and Naomi had a new hip.

Yes, the wind still blows.

○ ○ ○

The pastor and wife have an open-door, open-house, open-heart policy.

○ ○ ○

2001. Revisit with me the pile of worn sandals by the front door of the Dominion Road parsonage. The pastor and wife now living in that home have an open-door, open-house, open-heart policy. There are no less than 10 people eating and/or sleeping there every day. The pastor states his philosophy: "We believe in investment in mission, giving whoever will come an opportunity to see how a normal family with Christian values functions in today's world. Some people see all these people traipsing in and out as a negative thing, but it isn't."

I have to agree. It seems they are modeling Christ's invitation, "Come, and I will give you rest" and "Whosoever will may come and drink freely of the water of Life."

The 36-year-old pastor, Vipul Kharat, has pastored the first Church of the Nazarene in New Zealand, now called All Nations Church of the Nazarene, for seven years.

"My call is to cross-cultural ministry," Vipul says, "so the new name perfectly describes what our

Pastor Kharat of All Nations Church of the Nazarene

church tries to do to relate to contemporary society. Increased mobility in the world and widespread immigration demand change. We are reaching people who would never have let us near them in their own country, especially the 10-40 Window people groups. We must understand the God with a global heart."

What has laid the foundation for Vipul's zeal and philosophy of mission and prepared him for this ministry? "I was born in Bombay, India, to a Nazarene pastor's family," Vipul says, "but for years refused the Christian way. I wanted nothing to do with God and the church. While in university I committed my life to drugs, alcohol, and eastern religion. But in my final year while earning a degree in microbiology, I decided there had to be a God of the universe who masterminded this incredible creation. And if so, He was worthy of my worship and life devotion."

Vipul was discipled by Youth with a Mission and became an evangelist and leader of that group in the megalopolis of Bombay. Feeling the need for in-depth studies in God's Word, he enrolled in Australasian Nazarene Bible College in the early 1980s. After graduating he was planning to pastor a church there, but God used visa problems to send him to New Zealand.

○ ○ ○

Dad looked longingly over the thousands of red corrugated iron roofs and said, "Connie, that's our parish."

○ ○ ○

While helping with the church in Wainuiomata, near Wellington, he met his wife, Suzanne. They were married and returned to India to live—until a letter arrived. District Superintendent Byron Schortinghouse asked them to return to New Zealand to plant a church.

Vipul has indeed planted churches, and they have all been planted while pastoring the Dominion Road church. The Korean and Samoan congregations meet in the mother church building, while a multicultural church meets in an outlying area of Auckland.

Yes, the wind still blows.

○   ○   ○

2001. From a distance I can see One Tree Hill, a favorite place in the 1950s near Auckland for our family to retreat after a busy day. My mind takes me back through time.

The two-cylinder engine of our Jowett station wagon labored to climb the steep road that circled to the top of the volcanically formed landmark. From our vantage point high above the city we could see it all. The Pacific Ocean on one side and the Tasman Sea on the other in some places nearly pinched the land in two. It was quiet except for a few city sounds piercing enough to reach us. Dad looked longingly over the thousands of red corrugated iron roofs and said, "Connie, that's our parish."

That statement contained for me a twofold message. First, the responsibility of Christians to obey Christ's command to tell the Good News to every person was to be taken seriously. Second, I knew the word *our* included me in his and my mother's ministry.

Auckland, 2001

Sometimes friends would say, "Your parents are so strict or so fanatical. You'll reject their religion as soon as you can." Even though a child, I would shake my head. I knew then, even if only in part, the reality of a God that cuts through the failures of humans and the inequities of humankind's belief systems to show love and grace. And to Him I desired to be faithful.

○ ○ ○

2001. I made it! I have driven a borrowed car from Remuera to Mission Bay on the left side of the road without mishap. Thank You, Lord! I'm here to enjoy the sights and sounds of the beach and let my memories wander back through time.

Go back with me to a summer Sunday in 1957. I'm 13 years old, but the beach missions started long before that. My parents have driven our vehicle, as

Service at Mission Bay

they do every Sunday, crammed with church people and musical instruments to Mission Bay for an open-air service. Mother's marimba playing soon piques the curiosity of the sunbathers. They have seen xylophones, but this instrument has wooden keys. When the crowd has gathered, my father begins to tell why we are there. As he tells the age-old story of life and hope in Christ, some leave, uninterested in "that religious tripe," but others stay. There is singing of gospel songs and choruses, maybe a duet or a trio, a chalk sermon drawn by Maisie Davis, and testimonies interspersed throughout.

What has replaced the beach missions of the 1950s in the attempt to follow the apostle Paul's example when he said, "That by all means we might save some"?

2001. Tonight I'm speaking to a cross-cultural group in a home meeting. There are people of East Indian, European, Asian, and Fijian backgrounds. Their ages range from 6 to 60. Most are new believers with maybe one or two who have not yet believed. The singing, led by a vibrant young man, is enthusiastic and sincere. There are testimonies of praise to God and requests for prayer.

Now it is my turn to speak. I share the verses that continually challenge my life. "Whoever finds his life will lose it, and whoever loses his life for my sake will find it" (Matt. 10:39).

I wonder what chord has been struck in the hearts of these people with so much depth in their dark eyes? Is the Holy Spirit calling more laborers to the harvest from this place? How many pastors and layleaders? Pastor Vipul tells me there are home groups like this meeting almost every night of the week in different areas of Auckland. There are already 3 church plants; his dream is 10.

From beach missions to home groups. The settings are different. The beat of God's heart is the same.

The wind still blows.

Epilogue
Weather Forecast—Gray Skies or Blue?

I trust I've not painted such a rosy picture of the victories that you're not aware of the myriad battles for each win. In every land the battle is obvious to those with eyes to "see" in the spiritual realm, and the New Zealand field is no exception. I asked pastors and church leaders, "How must we pray? What are the great needs and issues in the Land of the Long White Cloud and how do they impact the church?"

They responded:

- The majority of people feel no need of God.
- Our society is becoming characterized by individualism, selfishness, and greed.
- Materialism and the New Age Movement have had a huge impact on the people of European descent, while the Maori religion, polytheism, and pantheism rolled together is a natural fit with New Age ideology.
- Political correctness and privacy have become an obsession. For example, if a person is prayed for publicly when they're not in the room, it can be ruled an invasion of privacy.
- The Church of the Nazarene is not immune from these influences, and the message of ho-

liness is not generally well-received by either the persons in the street or in the pew.

- In the early days, the church produced people who were willing to give their all for Christ and the building of His church. But now we seem so professional. Where is the fire?

○ ○ ○

Wesley said, "Prayerless pews, powerless pulpits."

○ ○ ○

What can the church do to meet the challenges? Again, the pastors and church leaders said:

- See the need for holy living and sacrificial service.
- Reject the popular lifestyles of comfort and wealth.
- Engage in spiritual warfare by a vital personal prayer life, brought about by a heart-thirst for God. Wesley said, "Prayerless pews, powerless pulpits."

In spite of the negative influences that abound there is cause for rejoicing. In these times of insecurity and uncertainty, people appear less complacent and self-satisfied. They seemingly are more spiritually aware, more open and responsive to the gospel. In particular, new immigrants to New Zealand appear willing to receive the Christian message and become involved in the community of faith. The field is white unto harvest.

I invite you—in fact, I urge you—to join me in praying for this special land. Would you pray that

- pastors and laypeople will be Spirit-filled and Spirit-led
- the indigenous church will rely on God as its source
- Nazarenes will model the holiness lifestyle and, as a result, impact the culture and catch the vision of a mighty God seeking to save the lost

On behalf of the Church of the Nazarene in New Zealand, I thank you for your prayers. Though Aotearoa is geographically under the globe our united international prayer force can "overcome the world." Praise the Lord!

Pronunciation Guide

Aorangi	ay-oh-RANG-ee
Aotearoa	ay-oh-TEH-ah-ROH-ah
Auckland	AWK-luhnd
Balmoral	bal-MOHR-uhl
Bentham	BEHN-thuhm
Bharat Bhanabais	bah-RAHT bahn-ah-BIE
Büsingen	BOO-zihn-guhn
Chevalier	sheh-vuh-LEER
Cor and Miep Holleman	KORH and MEEP HAH-luh-muhn
dinkum	DEEN-kuhm
Faataape	fah-ah-TAH-ah-peh
Hartlepool	HAHRT-luh-pool
Invercargill	ihn-ver-KARH-gihl
Kaio	KIE-oh
Kiwi	KEE-wee
Kudjip	KOO-djihp
Maori	MAU-ree
Mika	MEE-kuh
Nikolao	NIHK-oh-lau
Niue	NOO-ee
Pakeha	PAH-kee-hah
Papakura	pap-uh-KYOO-rah
Piha	PEE-hah
Remuera	reh-myoo-EH-rah
Ronnekamp	RAH-nee-kamp
Sepik	SEE-pihk

Tamaki	TAM-uh-kee
Tonga	TAHN-gah
Vipul Kharat	WEE-pool kah-RAHT
Wainuiomata	wie-NYOO-ee-oh-MAH-tah
Whangarei	FAHNG-ah-ray
Yearbury	YEER-boo-ree